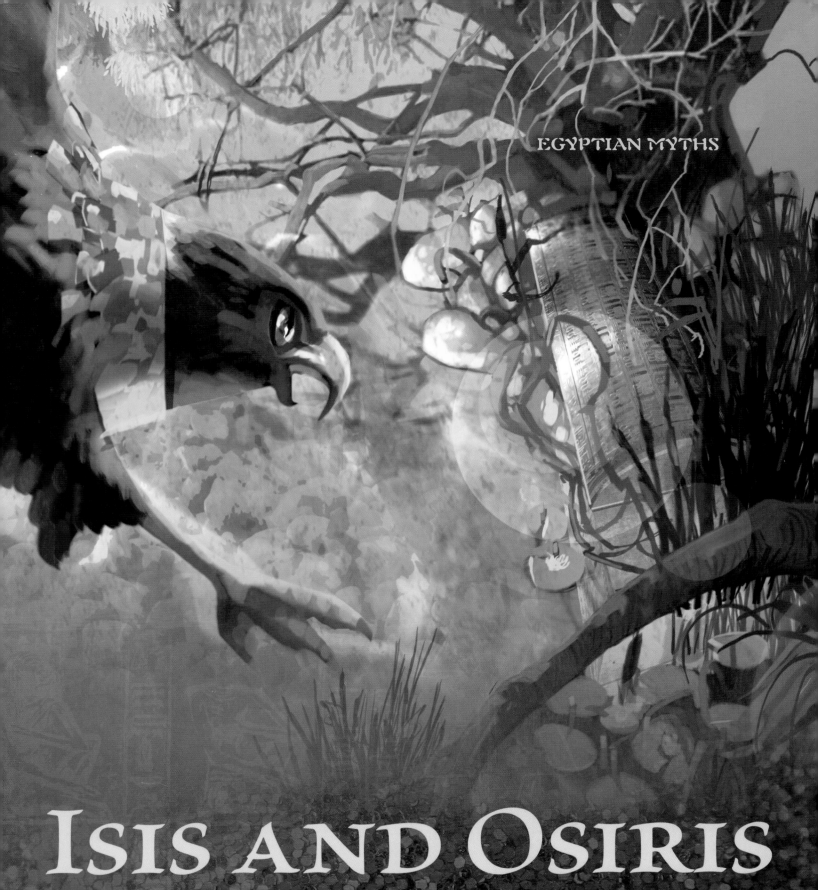

ISIS AND OSIRIS

A RETELLING BY CARI MEISTER ILLUSTRATED BY FRANCESCA D'OTTAVI

PICTURE WINDOW BOOKS
a capstone imprint

CAST OF CHARACTERS

Atum (AH-tuhm): the creator god; father of Tefnut and Shu

Tefnut (TEF-nut): goddess of moisture; sister to Shu

Shu (SHOO): god of the air; brother to Tefnut

Geb (GEHB): god of the earth; brother to Nut

Nut (NUT): goddess of the sky; sister to Geb

Osiris (oh-SIRE-is): god of the underworld; brother of Isis, Set, and Nephthys; husband of Isis

Isis (EYE-sis): goddess of magic and life; sister of Osiris, Set, and Nephthys; wife of Osiris

Set (SET): god of the desert and storms; brother of Isis, Nephthys, and Osiris; husband of Nephthys

Nephthys (NEF-theez): goddess of divine assistance; sister of Set, Osiris, and Isis; wife of Set

Horus (HOAR-us): god of the sky; son of Isis and Osiris

Thoth (THOTH): god of wisdom

WORDS TO KNOW

afterlife—the place where Egyptians believed a person's soul went after death

avenge—to get even for something

crook—an instrument held by ancient Egyptian rulers; it represents the shepherd of the people

embalm—to preserve a dead body from decay

flail—an instrument held by ancient Egyptian rulers; it represents the punishments necessary to maintain peace

mummify—to preserve a body with special salts and cloth to make it last a long time

pharaoh—a king of ancient Egypt

ACCORDING TO EGYPTIAN MYTH,

in the beginning there was only the god Atum. He was all-powerful, but he was lonely. So he created Tefnut and Shu to keep him company. Tefnut and Shu had two children: Geb, the god of the earth; and Nut, the goddess of the sky.

Geb and Nut had four children: Osiris, Isis, Set, and Nephthys. Osiris was the favored son and became pharaoh of Egypt.

Osiris was a wise and good leader, and his people flourished along the Nile's banks. Isis became Osiris' wife, and they ruled Egypt in harmony.

Set married his sister Nephthys. Set was strong and courageous. He battled fierce demons and won. But Set was jealous of Osiris.

"Why should Osiris get all the glory?" Set wondered. "I can rule just as well as he can."

So Set thought of a plot—an evil plot to destroy his brother and take the throne.

Returning from a three-month journey, Osiris strode into the palace. He was welcomed by all, including his beautiful wife, Isis. He greeted everyone warmly, but he was tired from his journey and longed to rest. Isis led him away from the crowd and into their private chambers.

"I'm so glad you're home. Rest for a moment," said Isis. "But I'm afraid it will be a short rest. Set has planned a grand party to celebrate your return."

Osiris studied his wife. "Set? Our brother?" he asked. "Don't you think he is evil?"

Isis bit her lip. "Yes. I don't trust him."

"Don't worry, Isis," said Osiris. "I'm sure everything will be fine."

While Osiris rested, Set made sure everything was ready for the banquet.

"Only one last thing to prepare," said Set. He went to an adjoining room, where his special gift for Osiris had been placed. His eyes widened as he studied the chest. The top was decorated with gold and jewels.

Set's fingers traced the carvings bordering the sides of the chest. "Yes!" he said. "This is the finest chest ever made. Too bad I won't see it for long."

Set raised his hand. As he chanted powerful magical words, the chest started to glow. An evil spell was cast.

Set smiled. "Now it is ready," he said.

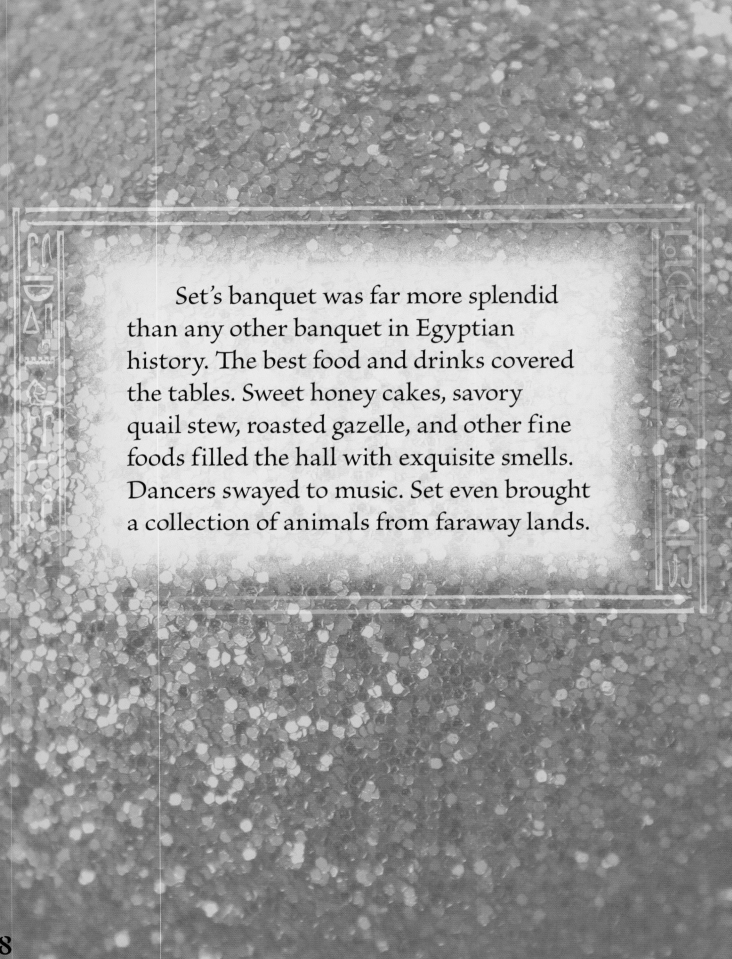

Set's banquet was far more splendid than any other banquet in Egyptian history. The best food and drinks covered the tables. Sweet honey cakes, savory quail stew, roasted gazelle, and other fine foods filled the hall with exquisite smells. Dancers swayed to music. Set even brought a collection of animals from faraway lands.

Osiris was delighted. "You have outdone yourself, Set!" he said. "This is a magnificent homecoming. Thank you, brother, for your kindness."

Set smiled. "There is one more surprise."

"Is that so?" asked Osiris. "Enlighten us, please."

Set waved to the guards. "Bring it in!" he commanded.

Ten guards carried in the chest, to the delight of all in the room.

"It's so marvelous!" said Osiris.

Set hushed the guests. "The man who can fit just perfectly into the chest can keep it!" he said.

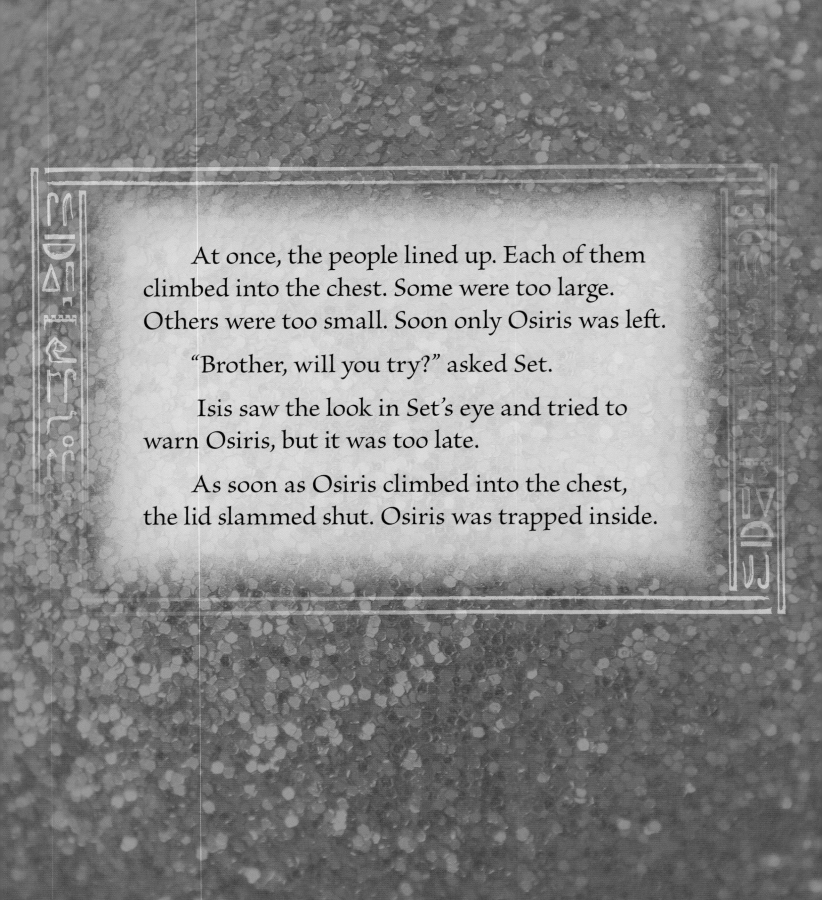

At once, the people lined up. Each of them climbed into the chest. Some were too large. Others were too small. Soon only Osiris was left.

"Brother, will you try?" asked Set.

Isis saw the look in Set's eye and tried to warn Osiris, but it was too late.

As soon as Osiris climbed into the chest, the lid slammed shut. Osiris was trapped inside.

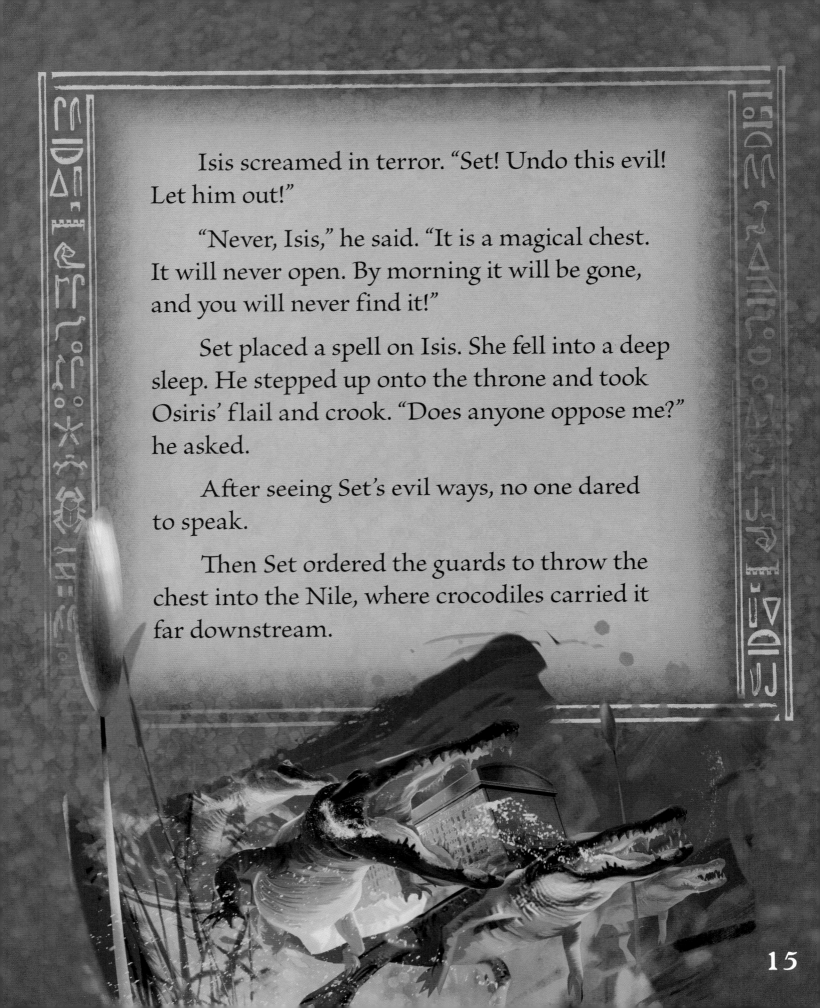

Isis screamed in terror. "Set! Undo this evil! Let him out!"

"Never, Isis," he said. "It is a magical chest. It will never open. By morning it will be gone, and you will never find it!"

Set placed a spell on Isis. She fell into a deep sleep. He stepped up onto the throne and took Osiris' flail and crook. "Does anyone oppose me?" he asked.

After seeing Set's evil ways, no one dared to speak.

Then Set ordered the guards to throw the chest into the Nile, where crocodiles carried it far downstream.

In the morning Isis woke early. She turned herself into a bird and flew away from the palace. She searched and searched, but she could not find the chest that held her husband.

Many years passed, but Isis did not give up. She traveled, sometimes as a bird and sometimes as a woman, farther and farther along the river.

One day, along the banks of the Nile, Isis saw a tall tree growing. She shivered and said, "Osiris is here!"

By the roots of the great tree, she found the chest containing Osiris' body. Using magic, Isis flew the chest home. But she did not go to the palace. Instead, she hid the chest in the reeds.

"I must keep it out of Set's hands," she said.

17

When Isis knew the chest was safe, she opened it with magic. Then she breathed life into Osiris and changed back into a woman.

Osiris woke and took his wife's hand. "I cannot stay in this world for long," he said. "But do not weep. When you wake, you will have my son growing inside you. His name will be Horus. He will avenge my death and rule Egypt in my place."

Isis lay down, closed her eyes, and fell asleep peacefully next to her husband. When she woke, Osiris was no longer breathing. Isis placed her hand on her belly, and she knew what Osiris had said was true.

That afternoon Isis locked the lid with magic and covered up the chest in the reeds. She needed to talk to the great god Thoth about giving Osiris a proper burial.

While she was away, Set went out hunting. He was chasing an antelope when he came to a large pile of reeds. "What is this?" he wondered as he brushed aside the reeds. "The chest!"

Set quickly looked around. Isis was nowhere to be seen. He motioned to his soldiers. "Come quickly," he said. "I wish for you to witness my strength."

The soldiers watched as Set used magic to open the chest. Osiris' body rose out of the chest and split apart into many pieces. The pieces were magically whisked away in different directions.

Set collapsed in exhaustion. "Go find Isis and tell her what I have done!" he said.

When Isis learned what Set had done, she cried in sorrow. "Evil Set! How could you be so cruel? This is not over. I will search all the land until I find every piece of my husband!"

Isis convinced her sister, Nephthys, to travel with her on her quest. Although Nephthys was Set's wife, she willingly helped Isis, because she knew Set's evil heart.

In time Isis gave birth to Horus. That day, she stared lovingly at her baby and said, "One day, my child, you will grow strong and avenge your father!"

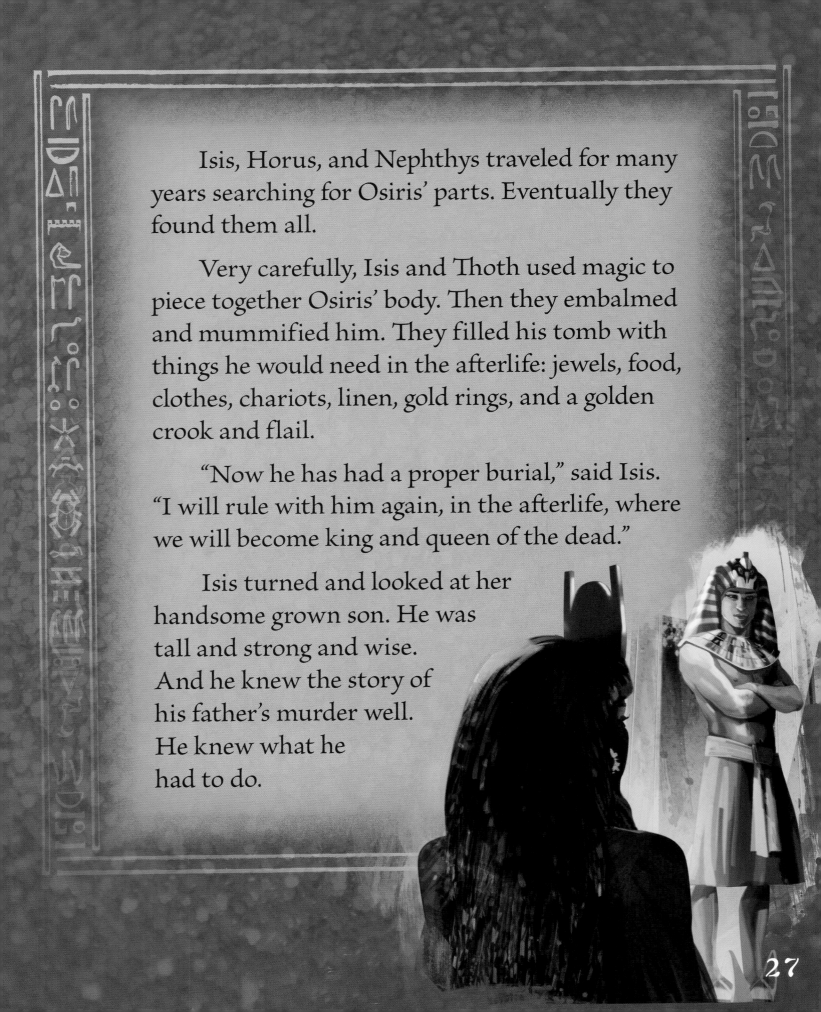

Isis, Horus, and Nephthys traveled for many years searching for Osiris' parts. Eventually they found them all.

Very carefully, Isis and Thoth used magic to piece together Osiris' body. Then they embalmed and mummified him. They filled his tomb with things he would need in the afterlife: jewels, food, clothes, chariots, linen, gold rings, and a golden crook and flail.

"Now he has had a proper burial," said Isis. "I will rule with him again, in the afterlife, where we will become king and queen of the dead."

Isis turned and looked at her handsome grown son. He was tall and strong and wise. And he knew the story of his father's murder well. He knew what he had to do.

Almost immediately after his father's burial, Horus challenged Set's claim to the throne. They fought for 80 years.

One of their greatest battles took place in the Nile River, where Set challenged Horus to a contest.

"Horus," he said, "let's turn ourselves into hippos. The first hippo to surface shall surrender the throne!"

The two men magically turned themselves into hippos. They thrashed underwater. Great waves splashed onto shore. But people watching the battle could not see who was winning.

After more than a week, the battle was even. Both hippos eventually surfaced at the exact same time. Neither of them was the winner of Set's contest.

29

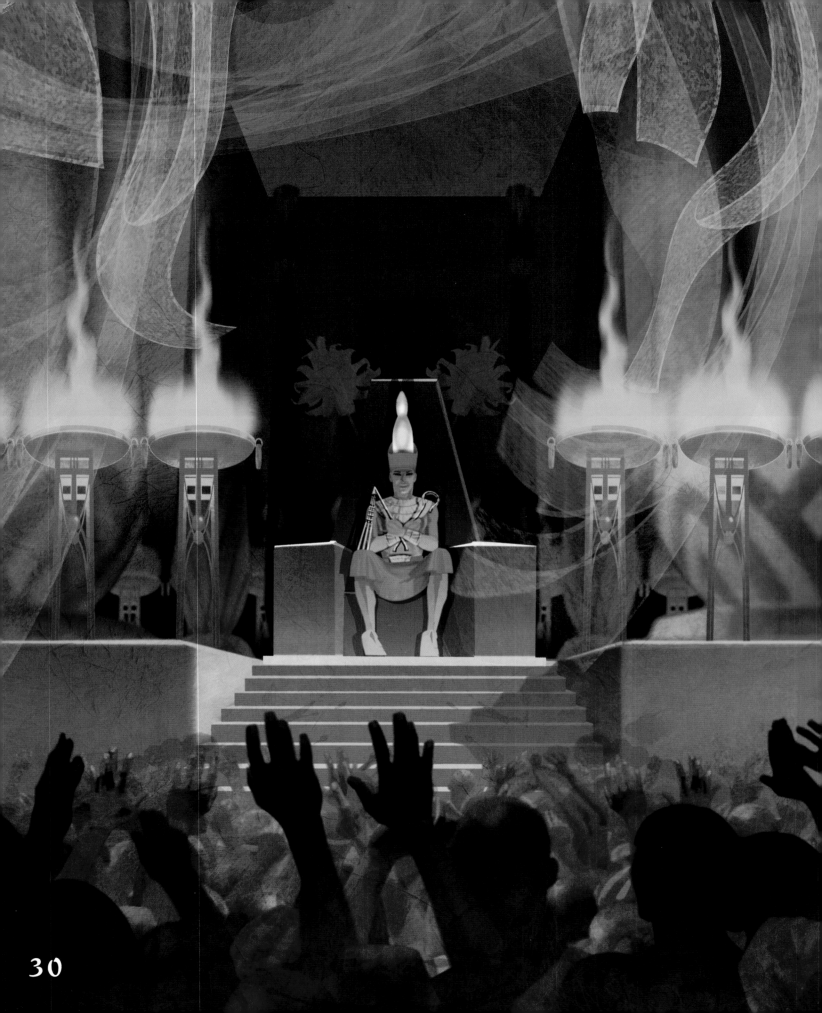

Eventually the older gods of Egypt grew weary of Set and Horus' battles over the throne.

"We must meet and decide their fate," said Geb, god of the earth.

Some of the gods favored Set. Some gods favored Horus. But in the end, Horus won the throne.

"Horus shall rule because he was the firstborn son of Osiris," commanded Geb.

Horus finally took the flail and crook and sat on his father's throne, where he ruled Egypt with kindness and strength. And as for Set, Horus banished him to the desert, where he wandered forever.

READ MORE

Bell, Michael, and Sarah Quie. *Ancient Egyptian Civilization.* Ancient Civilizations and Their Myths and Legends. New York: Rosen Central, 2010.

Elgin, Kathy. *Egyptian Myths.* Myths From Many Lands. New York: Skyview Books, 2009.

Limke, Jeff. *Isis and Osiris: To the Ends of the Earth.* Graphic Myths and Legends. Minneapolis: Graphic Universe, 2007.

INTERNET SITES

FactHound offers a safe, fun way to find Internet sites related to this book. All of the sites on FactHound have been researched by our staff.

Here's all you do:

Visit *www.facthound.com*

Type in this code: 9781404871489

 Super-cool stuff! Check out projects, games and lots more at
www.capstonekids.com

LOOK FOR ALL THE BOOKS IN THE EGYPTIAN MYTHS SERIES:

Thanks to our adviser for his expertise and advice:
Terry Flaherty, PhD
Professor of English
Minnesota State University Mankato

Editor: Shelly Lyons
Designer: Ted Williams
Art Director: Nathan Gassman
Production Specialist: Danielle Ceminsky
The illustrations in this book were created with watercolors, gouache, acrylics, and digitally.
Artistic Effects
Shutterstock: Goran Bogicevic, Kristina Divinchuk, Shvaygert Ekaterina, Vladislav Gurfinkel

Picture Window Books
1710 Roe Crest Drive
North Mankato, MN 56003
www.capstonepub.com

 All books published by Picture Window Books are manufactured with paper containing at least 10 percent post-consumer waste.

Library of Congress Cataloging-in-Publication Data
Meister, Cari.
Isis and Osiris : a retelling / by Cari Meister ; illustrated by Francesca D'Ottavi.
    p. cm. — (Egyptian myths)
"A Capstone imprint."
ISBN 978-1-4048-7148-9 (library binding)
ISBN 978-1-4048-7240-0 (paperback)
1. Gods, Egyptian—Juvenile literature. 2. Goddesses, Egyptian—Juvenile literature. 3. Mythology, Egyptian—Juvenile literature. I. D'Ottavi, Francesca. II. Title. III. Series: Egyptian myths.
BL2450.G6M45 2012
299.3113—dc23
                                    2011025840

Printed in the United States of America in North Mankato, Minnesota.
062012   006791R